Valerie Turner

Published By Plum Tree Books © 2013 Valerie Turner
All rights reserved. All images are copyright of their respective owners. This book is protected under the copyright laws of the United Kingdom. Any reproduction or other unauthorised use of the material or artwork herein is prohibited without the express written permission of the author.

British Library Cataloguing in Publication Data
A catalogue record for this book is available from the British Library

First Edition: December 2014
ISBN: 978-1-78484-232-1 (hbk)
ISBN: 978-1-78484-233-8 (pbk)
ISBN: 978-1-78484-234-5 (ebk)

www.plumtreebooks.co.uk

Introduction

Write it down is what they said
All those thoughts inside your head
But do they *really* want to know
What silly things confound me so?
Like: why is it when I'm in bed
Songs and tunes run through my head?
When I'm awake I'll sing a word
It really is a mite absurd.

Every night my dreams are vivid
This waste of brain power makes me livid
I dream that I am tall and slim
Fleet of foot and sound of limb
Is it just a quirk of fate?
I'm four foot nine and overweight
But then in dreams it doesn't matter
If in fact I'm short and fatter.

Last night I dreamt about our cat
In shiny boots and bowler hat
And then in fear of any fuss
He jumped onto a passing 'bus
I ran behind as in a race
Saw him stop in just one place
He cried and jumped a building tall
It must have been a caterwaul!

So even if it takes a while
I'll jot down what makes me smile
Even serious thoughts in verse
Though that could prove to be much worse
And if I can I'll make a book
So that they all can take a look
And maybe I can charge a fee
And donate to a *charity*.

VALERIE TURNER

Story Time

Claude Goes To Sea

(A tale of Claude, the cheeky toy chimp)

Cheeky chimp Claude was feeling quite bored
And said, "I need some fun."
So by himself he jumped off the shelf
To see what could be done.

There were lots of toys for girls and boys
All on the playroom floor
Dolls and trains, a horse with reins
And a bear with a bandaged paw.

Claude said, "I would like a trip in a sailing ship
Across the sea so blue;"
So he took his coat, climbed aboard a boat
And set off to see the view.

He sailed for a while with a cheerful smile;
The clock said half past three.
He had taken a tin with biscuits in,
So now he said "time for tea."

He then had a drink and said, "now I think
It is time that I had a nap;"
He closed his bright eyes, settled down with small sighs
But forgot to look at the map.

The waves grew so high they were reaching the sky
The boat went this way and that;
Claude woke up with a fright, but try as he might
He could not help falling flat.

He sighted some land with palm trees and sand;
The waves washed him onto the shore.
He jumped from his boat, took his tin and his coat
And said, "I'll go sailing no more."

Claude sat on the beach when with a loud screech,
A parrot flew down by his side.
She said, with a squawk, "To save a long walk
I'll fly you back home for the ride."

"Oh yes please" said Claude,
"I've left my boat moored,
But I really don't fancy the sea."
"Hop on," said Claude's friend,
"We'll get home in the end;
Hold on just as tight as can be."

Very soon they were back,
Claude climbed down from the back
Of his new feathered friend called Polly.
He had enjoyed flying high
With the clouds in the sky
And thought the whole trip rather jolly.

Then Claude went to bed
And yawning he said,
"For now my adventures are done."
But we know our young friend,
'And I think in the end
His stories have hardly begun.

Claude Joins The Circus

Claude the chimp jumped up and down
A circus show had come to town
Clowns and jugglers, cowboys too
Children waited in a queue.

Lots of horses big and tall
Were put into a warm, dry stall
Claude looked on and with a sigh
Said," I'd like to ride a horse that high."

The evening show was soon to start
So through the tent flap Claude did dart
A big brown horse was standing by
With pricked up ears and shining eye.

"If I get on and then just sit
It wouldn't hurt this horse one bit."
So being careful all the time
On to the saddle Claude did climb.

The horse thought, "Must be time to go."
And started on the evening show
Claude thought, "Wow" and that's a fact,
"I'm part of this great circus act."

The horse first trotted round the ring
And Claude sat up just like a king
But then he started going faster
Claude was heading for disaster

He clung onto the horse's mane
He could not reach the leading rein,
"I really mustn't lose my grip,"
Claude thought as he began to slip.

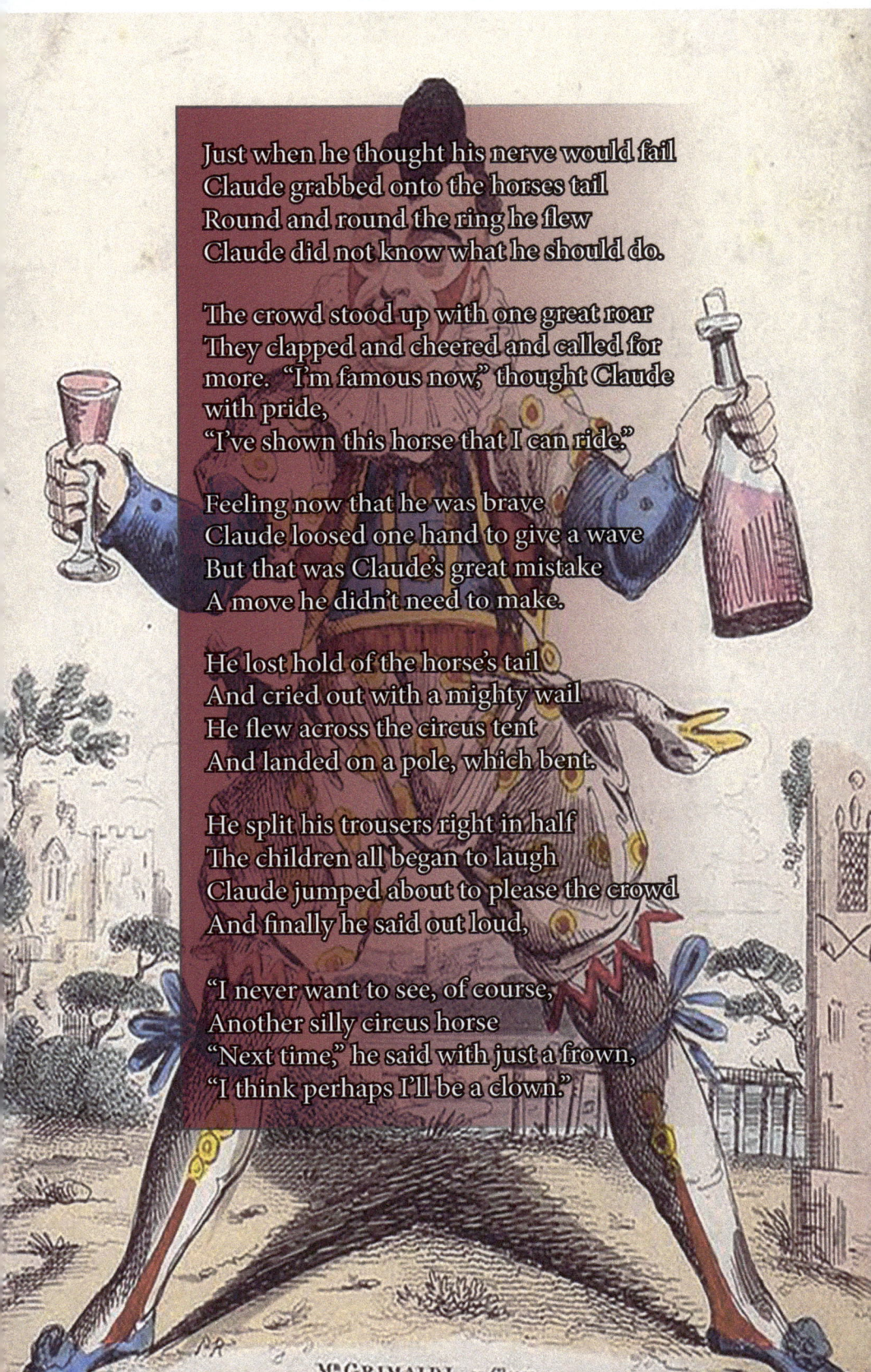

Just when he thought his nerve would fail
Claude grabbed onto the horses tail
Round and round the ring he flew
Claude did not know what he should do.

The crowd stood up with one great roar
They clapped and cheered and called for more. "I'm famous now," thought Claude with pride,
"I've shown this horse that I can ride."

Feeling now that he was brave
Claude loosed one hand to give a wave
But that was Claude's great mistake
A move he didn't need to make.

He lost hold of the horse's tail
And cried out with a mighty wail
He flew across the circus tent
And landed on a pole, which bent.

He split his trousers right in half
The children all began to laugh
Claude jumped about to please the crowd
And finally he said out loud,

"I never want to see, of course,
Another silly circus horse
"Next time," he said with just a frown,
"I think perhaps I'll be a clown."

Claude and the Scarecrow

Claude was in the countryside
Green fields spread from far and wide
Flowers were waving in the breeze
Birds were singing in the trees.

In a field right by a farm
Claude could see an outstretched arm
He ran as close by as he could
And said, "Hello, it's a man of wood."

His hair was made of yellow straw
His old coat nearly reached the floor
He had a carrot for a nose
He was supposed to scare the crows.

"Why do you stare?" The straw man said
And took the felt hat from his head.
"I know I look an awful fright
But I've been standing here all night!"

"I'd like to stretch my legs and walk."
"Oh" said Claude, "but you can talk!"
The scarecrow laughed and said, "Of course
So can the sheepdog and the horse.

I wonder if you would stay a while?"
Said the scarecrow with a smile.
"But watch out for those naughty crows
They sometimes land and peck your nose."

Claude climbed upon the scarecrow's stand
And soon the birds began to land.
"Go away – don't eat the crops
Leave the wheat and turnip tops!"

The birds pretended not to hear
Claude was not a chimp to fear
They pecked his shoes, undid his laces
While Claude was pulling funny faces.

"Go on. Shoo!" said Claude quite loud
The birds were making quite a crowd
Eating all the plants and seeds
Only leaving stones and weeds.

Just then the farmer walked right by
He hardly could believe his eye,
"Why are you just standing there?
These are the crows that you should scare!"

"I'll fetch the other scarecrow back
You are no use, you've got the sack."
"I'm jolly glad of that," said Claude,
"Standing still just makes me bored."

"I think I'll soon be on my way
Enough excitement for one day
I'm feeling thirsty now, I think
I'd like a biscuit and a drink."

Claude ran over to the gate
He said," I'm off, I can't be late
I think the time is after three
I'll just get home in time for tea."

A Woolly Tale

Hester Lester loved to knit
She couldn't get enough of it
She was a happy, homely girl
At her best with plain and purl.

Her needles they would click and clack
Hester had a knitter's knack
When the nights were drawing in
She got herself a fleece to spin.

Humming softly at her wheel
Spinning wool had its appeal
Her ever loving husband, Sid
Was quite bemused by what she did.

She wound her wool in balls and shanks
And even Sidney gained some thanks
For stretching wide his loving arms
So that she could wind her yarns.

Her knitting needles flew apace
You'd think it was some kind of race
She knitted Sidney socks and hats
And jackets for the neighbour's cats.

Scarves and mitts, egg cosies too
A cover for the downstairs loo
Outside the garden gnome looked plumper
Because he wore a knitted jumper.

Now Sidney caused a right palaver
For casting off his balaclava
He sought some solace in his shed
Where there were knitted cushions – red.

Said Sid, "I think I'll take a walk
And see if there are birds to stalk.."
He set off at a rapid pace
His long wool scarf around his face

Some while later Sid did see
An interesting looking tree
He climbed up to the treetop tall
Taking care not to fall.

But when the branch did start to curve
Poor Sidney really lost his nerve,
"I can't climb down; I've lost my grip."
His heart began to do a flip.

Then he had a clever thought
Before he really got too fraught
He unwound his scarf and with a wail
Tied it so he could abseil.

As poor Sid wound round and round
He lowered gently to the ground
He gave a nervous little laugh
And said, "Thank goodness for my scarf."

He scuttled home to be with Hester
No longer would her knitting pester
'Cos really when you look at it
She saved the fate of this (k)nit wit.

So in the evening firelight rosy
Hester knitted one more cosy
While Sidney faked contented sighs
He'd pulled the wool over her eyes.

The Ballad of "Chutney Jim"

"Chutney" Jim loved to cook
Taught himself without a book
Sometimes he thought his finest hour
Was when his arms were deep in flour.

He started simple, then progressed
He wanted folks to be impressed
His natural love for all things edible
Produced some dishes quite incredible.

His family were quite used to Jim
Indulged him in his every whim
And on waking in their beds
Often smelt his new baked bread.

He made them pies and cakes and roasts
And such exotic Melba toasts
His pasta dishes from the pan
Would do him credit in Milan.

His Sunday lunch was no mean feat
The tenderest of all roast meat
His crispy crackling was sublime
And pleased his guests time after time.

But then young "chutney" got his chance
He was to take a trip to France
Where they produced the confiture
That had a reputation pure.

"I can't compete with that," said Jim
And then an idea came to him
Perhaps French taste buds he could tickle
With just a taste of Jimmy's pickle.

He gathered jars of many sizes
Enough to reach right to Devizes
Some were large and others tiny
He washed them all till they were shiny.

Jim gathered all the surplus veg
And piled it on the kitchen ledge
He diced and sliced and chopped and pared
Visitors just stood and stared.

Frying, boiling, poaching, steaming
Young Jim's life took on new meaning
Filling jars and writing labels
He spread his wares across the tables.

When he crossed the village square
People stopped to sniff the air,
"What's that perfume?" They would ask,
"Vintage vinegar from the cask."

Soon Jim's fame began to grow
He featured at the produce show
His chutney knocked the judges silly
They couldn't cope with Jimmy's chilli.

People flocked from far and wide
His family was filled with pride
Who would think this little fella
Could outshine that lass Nigella?

Jim soon became a TV star
With mansion house and fancy car
Gourmet chefs with tempting dishes
Waited by to meet his wishes.

But although it was most pleasant
Eating partridge, duck and pheasant
Jim's joy was going back to Putney
For a hunk of cheese – with chutney.

The Disgruntled Fairy

The fairy on the Christmas tree
Gave a yawn and said, "Dear me
It's that certain time of year
When I get to stay up here.

I'm held up by a piece of wire
They couldn't get me up much higher
When I see the floor below
I get a touch of vertigo.

I sometimes wish they'd change things round
And put me somewhere near the ground
The only problem though with that
You get a sniff from their old cat.

The middle branches are more roomy
But down there it is quite gloomy
Up here I've got a fairy light
Darned thing flashes day and night!

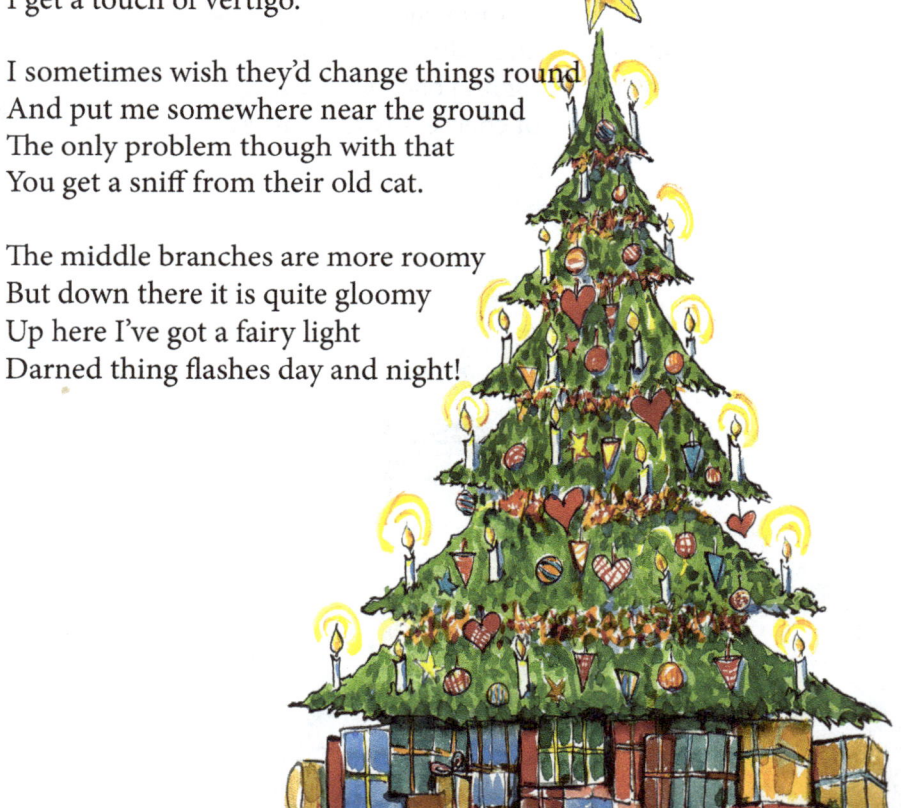

By HikingArtist

Don't they think I'd like a rest
From pine needles in my chest?
Balanced on this flimsy twig
They don't really care a fig.

A Santa on the branch quite near
Looked at me with festive leer
If I could just reach down below
I'd smack him in his 'ho–ho–ho.'

That snowman with his eyes of coal
Thinks himself a special soul
I'd soon remove his silly grin
And chuck his carrot in the bin.

There's that doll with airs and graces
Got one of those girly faces
All eyelashes, smiles and teeth
Wonder what she's like beneath?

        This year they've got a wooden clown
        With arms that go right up and down
        He bangs them on a little drum
        Just to make my poor ears hum.

        Oh watch out! The kids are here
        Wonder what they'll do this year?
        Must admit it was quite funny
        When they ate the chocolate bunny.

They always give the tree a shake
To see what mess they all can make
They sometimes poke my fairy wand
I'd wish them in the garden pond.

Oh, not the Grandma, just the same
Always calls me by her name
Reminds her of her little girl
With big blue eyes and golden curl.

Still - I suppose it's not all bad
There are worse jobs to be had
The Christmas turkey met his fate
And ended trussed up on a plate.

So I'll twinkle from afar
Bless them with my shiny star
And when I go back in the box
I hope that Santa's changed his socks."

Vintage Girl

They say she's a vintage shop junkie
A regular seen at the till
From glass beads to a special stuffed monkey
All waiting to give her a thrill.

She has fun sorting through all the 'knick-knacks.'
The unknown that could make her day
The painted egg with the jewels on
Could possibly be Fabergé.

The boxes of jewellery – broken
Can soon get her heart in a whirl
Amidst the glass and the plastic
There might be a genuine pearl.

Need to check on those bright patterned tea cups
A little bit gaudy you see
But it could be that everyone's missed it
A design by the great Clarice C.

Here and there a discarded handbag
With stories they never can tell
They've been seen in all the best places
Are they really by Coco Chanel?

The taffeta gown in the corner
A beautiful pale dusky pink
Did it go to an elegant party
With maybe a lady in mink?

What's the tale of the broken tiara?
A giggly young girl at her prom
Coming home with her streaky mascara
Ready for facing her mom.

What of the gold strappy sandals
With heels that defy you to walk?
They might be the source of some scandals
Oh how we wish they could talk.

Records that are now outdated
Playing jazz, blues and great rock 'n' roll
The sounds of the 60's were rated
Music that came from the soul.

Baby clothes no longer wanted
Jigsaws she hopes are complete
Bath salts (from aunty at Christmas)
Something to soothe aching feet.

A teddy with eyes so appealing
Casually thrown on a rack
His face turned to stare at the ceiling
He just needs a pat on the back.

The quest for treasure - non-ending
A search for an item unique
Wait – what's that vase on the shelf there?
Do you think it could be by Lalique?

Vintage girl keep on seeking good fortune
The rainbow must have an end
Your crock of gold may be waiting
The next shop is just round the bend.

Pets & Other Animals

Birdwatching

I like to watch the garden birds
Won't bore you now with flowery words
But suddenly I hear a rustle
Birds fly off, all hustle bustle.

In the hedgerow lying low
Hoping that his coat won't show
Neighbour's cat is slyly lurking
His camouflage is almost working

I challenge him by clapping hands
But now defiantly he stands
With haughty tail high in the air
He fixes me with baleful stare.

He's a furry purry fat cat
Should be on the mat cat
Couldn't chase a rat cat
A sort of this and that cat
May like a little pat cat
Perhaps a friendly chat cat
But that's enough of that cat
For now – just run and scat cat!

Cat Antics

Thunderball the ginger cat
Is getting old and far too fat
He sat upon the garden wall
And thought, "I'll not do much at all."

A pecking bird hove into view
"I s'pose there's something I must do,"
Said Thunderball whilst staying still
The blackbird filled his yellow bill.

"I'm meant to run and chase that bird
But really that is quite absurd
I'll chase him then he'll fly away
And they'll be laughing anyway.

I'll glance behind me, are they looking?
No, busy in the kitchen cooking
I'll fix the bird with angry stare
He doesn't seem to know I'm there.

I'll slip quite quietly to the ground
Make sure that no one is around
Pop back inside – my usual place
My window seat – no loss of face!

Ferdinand The Feisty Frog

Ferdinand the feisty frog
Lay in the pond just like a log
Through the days of snow and ice
To venture out was far from nice.

The owner of the pond was Geoff
Who, rumour said, was far from deaf
So he heard a feeble croak
When he popped outside to smoke.

In case old Ferdy's days weren't done
He'd left his waterfall to run
He thought it through and that was nice
So Ferdy didn't turn to ice.

When the ice and snow did clear
There was music to Geoff's ear
Vaguely through the thickening fog
He saw the outline of a frog.

"Well I never..." Geoff did tell,
"Ferdy is alive and well
He's trying hard to get a grip
The pond's cold sides give him the slip.

He wants to climb out and explore
Search for food where there is more
But all his efforts seem in vain
His energy will start to drain."

So kindly Geoff searched round the ground
'Till a little spade he found
Folks may think he's going madder
But he made his frog a ladder!

So feisty Ferdy can escape
From the confines of his lake
And when we hear a hearty croak
It's thanks to Geoff, a real nice bloke.

(Geoff says he thinks it is a toad
But I'm not going down that road)

It's Snow Joke

Thunderball the ginger cat
Cried quite loudly from the mat
"Open the door – I must go
What's this silly stuff called snow?

It's lying thick outside the door
I'll touch it gently with my paw
I don't like that, it feels too cold
To venture out would be so bold.

I'll jump onto the garden wall
Sitting here I seem quite tall
But how to get along the path
They are watching, I'm sure they'll laugh.

I try to move with usual swagger
I give them looks like a dagger
I sink into the fluffy stuff
I'm going back I've had enough.

The master's cleared a path to walk
I sometimes wish that I could talk
It doesn't lead to where I go
You'd think by now that he would know.

I prick my ears then take a leap
And land in what is quite a heap
It's cold right to my shoulder tops
I wish I'd got some thermal socks.

I struggle on, the pace is slow
But up the garden I must go
I round the corner, do my duty
I don't see the sparkling beauty.

My paws make patterns in the snow
Because it's deep I'm very slow
At last I'm at the kitchen door
"Come in," they say," and wipe your paws."

But now I'm on my window seat
Paws are folded nice and neat
I look a picture, that I know
'Ginger cat reflects on snow.'

Lazy Days

Bluebells ripple in the breeze
New leaves flutter in the trees
Wallflowers waft their heady scent
People smile, they are content.

Birds are chirping, seeking food
Peaceful is the general mood
But wait – what's in the hedge to spy
Sunlight on an amber eye?

Lying still behind the flowers
Prepared to stay for many hours
Daffodils mask golden coat
Silently cat sits to gloat.

He waits and looks out to the lawn
Sometimes gives a sleepy yawn
Will a hapless bird stray by
Not see the glint of steely eye?

Cat's days of running fast are done
He'd rather slumber in the sun
But now and then he feels the need
To show he still can move at speed.

Sometimes he checks to see if "they"
Are watching him as is their way
In case he sees a bird to chase
And misses it - with loss of face.

The sun gets higher in the sky
Lazily he swats a fly
He'll squint his eyes and have a peep
But very soon he's fast asleep.

And when the day draws to a close
The smell of dinner tweaks his nose
He'll yawn and stretch and then be fed
Before a rest – and then to bed.

Ode To A Ginger Cat

Oh ginger cat we're in your thrall
What do you think about us all?
You view us all with sphinx like stare
I wonder, do you really care?

You give a cry, we're by your side
Your amber eyes you open wide.
"Care for biscuits, food or drink?"
I wonder what you really think?

Sometimes we know it's time to play
Fetch out the toys that were away
Lie on the floor, play to your fad
I wonder, do you think we're mad?

And when it's time for you to rest
You put us to our final test
Open doors, make up the bed
I wonder what is in your head?

Oh ginger cat we're in your thrall
For you enchant us one and all
What are your thoughts on all above?
We're motivated by our love.

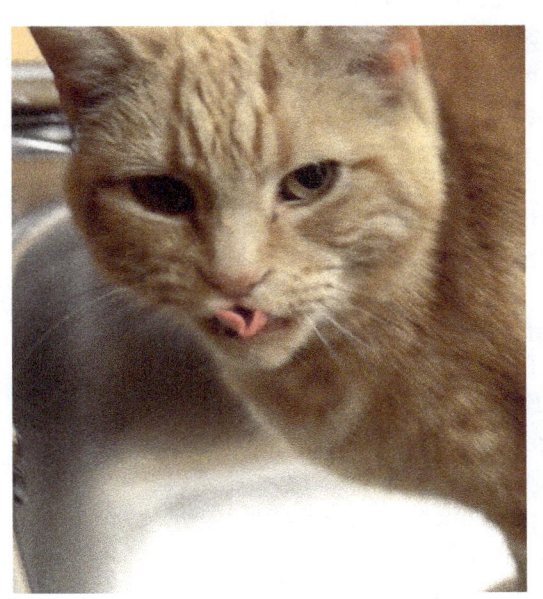

Old Man Ginger

The ginger cat is growing old
A fact that makes my blood run cold
His frailty is now on view
And there is nothing we can do.

A coat that once was fiery red
Glows a gentle gold instead
Where he had a strident miaow
His vocal chords are muted now.

Despite being given cuts so tender
His fragile frame is yet more slender
He climbs the stairs with measured tread
Where once he ran and leaped ahead.

He quietly pads across the floor
Wonders what he's come in for
Appears as in a confused state
A fact to which I can relate!

He likes to find a cosy place
And lie with sunshine on his face
A foolish bird flutters by
Cat watches him with rheumy eye.

He wanders to the house next door
And seeks out grandma – 94
No need for words they are as one
Harmoniously sitting in the sun.

When darkness falls he likes a nap
Curled up on his master's lap
But this deep sleep is just a tease
If you try to eat some cheese.

He has a clock inside his head
Which dictates the time for bed
Stay up late if you dare
Admonished with a steely stare.

He used to sleep inside the shed
But now prefers his master's bed
So on a towel laundered clean
He spreads himself quite serene.

No longer such a robust cat
But handsome still despite all that
I will remain his biggest fan
And treat him like a grand old man.

Peaceful Pals

The old man sits on garden bench
His face turned to the sun
He has finished now his morning's work
All his tasks are done.

The ginger cat strolls up the path
He has heard his master's voice
He takes his place at old man's feet
Of that there is no choice.

Harmonious in their search for peace
They sit without a word
No movement, just a feline glance
At some intrusive bird.

The man looks down at sleepy cat
Who raises up his head
A soft caress behind the ears
Will stand him in good stead.

Man and cat at one with life
Their true affection shows
No need for noise or nagging wife
Just leave them there to doze.

Nature

A Winter's Tale

I wake up on a wintry morn
And gaze in wonder at the lawn
Every blade is sparkling white
Almost as painted in the night.

The oak is bathed in golden glow
The winter sun puts on a show
Squirrels scamper at great speed
Storing nuts that they might need.

Garden plants stand stiff outside
As if they've all been petrified
A touch of colour here and there
Relieves the border from being bare.

Blackbirds squabble on the wall
There's food enough to feed them all
But each one wants a certain patch
No other piece of hedge will match.

The cat stalks by with careful gait
But once again he is too late
The birds fly off into next doors
He's left to lick his frozen paws.

To me it is a glorious view
Nature's magic that is true
But best of all the things I've said
Are seen in comfort from my bed!

In A Nutshell

Squirrel darting – hurry, scurry
Quicker now than Andy Murray
Busily his nuts he's shelving
Searching food, digging, delving

To and fro all hustle bustle
Through the hedge without a rustle
Almost makes your head go dizzy
Round and round he's in a tizzy

Up the tree – oh how fantastic
Would that I were that gymnastic
Though he's called a garden pest
As squirrels go – he is the best

Springtime In The Park

Springtime sunshine made its mark
And filtered through the leaves to park
We stopped and sat on wooden seats
And watched the ducks being fed their treats.

Leisurely they glide downstream
While we sit dozing half in dream
The goose, protective of his mate
Sees off his rival filled with hate.

Swans on bank have made a nest
They try to settle for some rest
But the peace of river palls
Torn by youthful raucous calls.

Young lads are larking in canoe
Being taught to row and what to do
For others kayaking is fun
Their oars bright glistening in the sun.

Office workers, pin-striped suits
Failing in their health pursuits
Walk briskly, flap identi-tags
Relaxing with illicit fags.

Some with iPods glued to ear
Lest the outside world they hear
Lycra clad they jog on by
Careful not to meet the eye.

Flashing by, a gleaming hull
Fit young men who've learned to skull
Skim silently as if on ice
Glorious sight, gone in a trice.

Silver heads on scooters meet
Not for them some busy street
Stopped midway through the morning run
To gossip in the gentle sun.

New leaves on the willow trees
Dapple paths in gentle breeze
Early blossom now on show
Looks like flakes of pale pink snow.

Round the playground toddlers shout
Released from chairs to play about
Mothers sporting summer tops
Exposing arms and shiny "mops."

When at last our thirst we quench
Seated at the cafe bench
A whiff of paint we soon detect
Springtime sprucing we suspect.

The thought of sunny days ahead
Past the winter that we dread
Keep on hoping that's the thing
And celebrate this time of spring.

Squeaky The Sparrow

Squeaky is a sparrow who visits every spring
We know the weather is warmer when he begins to sing
He starts to make a nest in the eaves above the door
And drops his twigs and feathers straight down upon the floor.

When decorating is finished in his twiggy bachelor pad
He starts to eye the "talent" to see what can be had
He settles down to business on our nearby garden gate
And lubricates his larynx for calling for a mate.

He starts to squeak quite loudly and never draws a breath
But everyone around him is deafened half to death
He starts at early morning - if you're lucky not till six
We groan and say, "Oh Squeaky is up to his old tricks."

It's not that we don't love him and wish him all the best
But please some sparrow lady come and share his nest
Occasionally he flies off and then peace reigns supreme
But soon he is back and squeaking – it makes you want to scream.

We've often been quite hopeful when a female hoves in view
And Squeaky entertains her 'cos he is hopeful too
But all too soon the squeaking starts in the upstairs gutter
He wasn't too successful we notice-with a mutter.

The days are getting long now and nightfall is quite late
But this won't stop young Squeaky from shouting for a mate
Just as we're getting desperate and don't know what to do
We see a sight to cheer us - not one bird, but two.

Let's hope this lady sparrow likes Squeaky's smart new nest
And thinks he looks quite handsome as he puffs his little chest
Please move in lady sparrow and make a home with chicks
I'll even stop complaining when you throw down mud and sticks.

    Be a proper family
        And keep the children quiet
            'Cos if they grow like Squeaky
                There could even be a riot
                    But when the evenings darken
                        And we lose the bow and arrow (!)
                          We know we're going to miss him
                            That squawking aqueaky sparrow

The Winter Garden

As I walk into the garden
On a wintry afternoon
The plants are dull and lifeless,
There's an atmosphere of gloom
The snow has done some damage
To flowers, which is quite sad
The shrubs have fared much better,
They don't seem so bad.

The path is wet and slimy
It's difficult to walk
Once brightly coloured, flower tubs
Are bearing just a stalk
The birds are looking hungry
The hedges stark and bare
Everything's neglected
As if we didn't care.

But as I look around me
I take a different view
In the sky there are some patches
Of really startling blue
Underneath the benches
I see some small green shoots
And know the springtime flowers
Are putting down their roots.

The days are getting longer,
The sun is not so low
There is still a lot of winter,
That I surely know
It's wrong to see the dullness,
Dead things and decay
Take note of all the pointers,
Spring is on its way.

Thoughts From Prawle Point

(South west coast path, Devon)

The soft sweet hum of lazy bees
The gentle stirring of the trees
The golden rays on glistening seas
What more could put the heart at ease?

The sweet perfume of roses wild
Remind me of my time as child
When by the world I was beguiled
And to my memory all was filed.

Yachts that bob across the blue
Ships not quite within my view
Peeping flowers of every hue
These are sights that soothe me too.

If all these things can be admired
In a world that's far too tired
And I feel my spirits hired
Then I have truly been inspired.

Wake Up Call

The fingers of the morning sun slowly stroke my face,
"Gently wake," they seem to say, "life is not a race."

I lie quite still and from my bed no raucous noise is heard
The only sound to reach my ear is singing of a bird.

The squirrel scampers from the tree and starts his search for food
But he is silent as can be and does not break the mood.

Flowers stand in muted rows awaiting hungry bees
A neighbour's washing on the line flutters in the breeze.

"Appreciate it while you can," the trees just seem to say
These moments are more precious than the ones in later day.

But then the dogs begin to bark, the peaceful mood has gone
Children shout and car doors bang. Stand by – the race is on!

Musings

A Certain Age

I need to ask a question
There's something I should know
When do I start announcing
"I'll soon be so and so?"

When I was just a toddler
And by my Mother's knee
I'd look at folks who asked me
And lisp, "I'm nearly free."

I went to school to learn things
And thought I was in heaven
I shared my worldly knowledge
I knew a lot at seven.

The teens are best glossed over
For then I knew it all
I'd try to look superior
Though not quite five foot tall.

I'd watch young children playing
With skipping ropes or bat
And sigh with a hint of longing
I'm far too old for that.

I'd mark each milestone birthday
And proudly tell my age
Parties, boys and dancing
Would soon become the rage.

Finally I reached it
The magic twenty one
The newspaper announced it
My life had just begun

As the years were added
A phrase that I used more
I'm glad I keep my age well
I'm only twenty four.

I sailed right through the thirties
I thought that they were fine
I started serious thinking
When I reached thirty nine.

The day that I was forty
To prove that I was young
I ran right up the garden
Though wheezing through my lung.

I coasted through my fifties
No need to shout my age
Just get a good hairdresser
Add colour, that's the rage.

When I got to sixty
A pension hove in view
So many things not done yet
So much more to do.

But when did I become
One of those senior folk
Who have to be quite careful,
When laughing at a joke.

And I can do my shopping
At any time of day
But it's more satisfying
To get in the worker's way.

I watch the television
And create about the sound
It's not clear as it used to be
More muffled I have found.

If I am like my parents
I've still a way to go
And am eager to be saying
"I'm ninety five you know!"

My ramblings are long winded
And fill page after page
But what you must remember
Is - I'm at that certain age.

Give Us A Break

He settles back into his chair
With a smile that's so serene
He watches the bright colours
That dance across the screen

The red of shiny apples
Polished till they glow
The pink of cherry blossom
 Like a fall of snow

The blue of seaside water
The brown of nutty hue
The black that shines like patent
On a pretty smart new shoe

The green of grass so dazzling
That's freshened by the rain
But what is all this splendour?
It's snooker time again!

Is It Me?

Is it me – or do they mumble, these actors on TV?
I sit to watch a programme with a nice hot cup of tea.

Eagerly I'm waiting for the drama to begin
But all is overshadowed by unnecessary din.

The characters start talking, the mood like music swells
I'll only ever hear them if somebody just yells.

Is it me – or do they whisper to make us listen hard
In quiet documentaries or something from the bard?

And even daily viewing of those infernal soaps
Gives shouting a new meaning and raises all our hopes.

I watch my favourite drama, see the heroine advance
Her sultry tones are muted, oh please give me a chance.

The hero gazes at her, she gives a little sigh
Oh come on dear please save me from turning volume high.

He whispers so profoundly, her eyelashes do flutter
But whatever is he saying? Speak up love, don't mutter.

I watch a quiz like programme, some wit makes an aside
My husband laughs quite loudly with glee he cannot hide.

He sees my set expression and thinks I'm feeling glum
When really I am struggling to hear – just like my mum.

Is it me – or do young folk ever speak
Or do they just do miming because they are too weak?

Should one of them address me – while texting on their phone
I can't keep saying, "Pardon?" Or they will start to moan.

This modern day affliction for background noise in shops
I certainly can hear that – in fact it never stops.

And when I do go shopping and finally make my choice
Why does the young assistant speak in a little voice?

The cat demands attention, he gives a faint meow
Sometimes he is just voiceless – he's getting older now!

So I'll just sit down quietly with another cup of tea
I've come to the conclusion it's them – it can't be me!

Knees Up

I wish I could sort out my knee
It's started bothering me
It squeaks, creaks and clicks
Invariably sticks
It's becoming a nuisance you see.

I don't ask a lot of this joint
Well really there isn't much point
Just get on and do
What I ask you to
While I with painkiller anoint.

It's never been one that I show
'cos I'm not a model you know
No short little skirts
That teases and flirts
It's just there to get up and go.

Oh occasionally I give it a treat
Pay attention to legs, knees and feet
Smooth in perfumed cream
That smells like a dream
Attempting to keep it quite sweet.

There's no (k)need for it to get in a huff
To blow up and be full of puff
I think very soon
I'll resemble a balloon
An end to this nonsense and stuff!

Oh I know I've put on extra weight
And I may have left it quite late
To slim down to size
In everyone's eyes
But it really should know that is fate.

I look in the mirror and see
A far from impressive right knee
No skin smooth as silk
Despite moisture milk
But wrinkled and old as can be.

Now medical help I did seek
After I had a bad week
The doc he did stab it
(Shan't make that a habit)
But still I continued to creak.

There are knees that are dimpled and cute
Fine for a modelling shoot
   But mine's not up there
   For people to stare
   At and say, "Goodness me what a beaut!"

So I'm launching a final appeal
To a knee that is failing to kneel
   Stop messing about
   And making me shout
   Get back to an even keel.

   I'm asking as just an old friend
   Enough now, just give in and bend
     It's just boring you see
     All this knee repartee
     So hopefully – this is the end!

Mr Somebody

I'm seeking Mr Somebody – I know that he exists
And if I ever find him I may just slap his wrists
So far I've been unlucky – he's proving so elusive
I get a certain feeling he's not just mine exclusive.

I know he's made a visit to see my good friend Jan
She told me so when chatting as only old friends can
Other friends have muttered that they know who I mean
Proof of his existence is all there to be seen.

Is he tall and handsome? Could he be quite rich?
I bet he's short and balding 'cos life can be a bitch
Does he watch me sleeping – am I safe at night?
'Though my purple bed socks would soon give him a fright.

Although we've not yet seen him we know he must be there
'Cos when we're all not looking he moves things from the chair
I'm worried he's light fingered – some objects go astray
Then he will return them on another day.

He probably wears glasses but hasn't got his own
He's known to move mine often when they were by the 'phone
He sometimes leaves doors open which we just know we locked
And when we come upon them we really are quite shocked.

So when your keys go missing from where they used to hang
And drawers are left wide open – you close them with a bang
It's that elusive person – it's never you or me
As we so often say now "it must be somebody!

School Run

Come and park your four by four
Opposite to our front door
All line up – the parking's free
 But hurry now it's almost three.

Usual space? – it's force of habit
Run to find it like a rabbit
Hope it goes without a hitch
No-one dares to steal your pitch.

Sit in silence in your cages
 Waiting now – it must seem ages
Read a book - you on your own?
Chat into your mobile phone.

Approaching the appointed hour
Someone above sends down a shower
Guaranteed to test you more
Superior in your four by four.

Open boot – what's your necessity?
Umbrella is a must accessory
Buggy for the youngest member
Rituals that you must remember.

Open door – unstrap the baby
Put him in his pushchair maybe
Toddler likes a bright pink scooter
Passing friends "pip" on a hooter.

Child rides high on Daddy's shoulder
Are the parents getting older?
Mummy in designer hat
Sometimes stops with friends to chat.

Teetering on their fashion heels
Waiting for the children's squeals
Blink an eye – they're coming back
Now it's time the car to pack.

Baby, buggy, scooter, bags,
"Mind the road, don't run," she nags
Difficult to keep a track
Lock them in – safe in the back.

Join the ritualistic herd
That they could walk has not occurred
It could be quicker in the end
But what message would that send?

Rain again – it's on the cards
Now drive home – five hundred yards
But at least you know the score
You've done it in your four by four.

Experiences

Canal Boats

A Sunday stroll beside the lock
Allowed me time to just take stock.
Of all the boats that passed or moored,
Some on the move, others stored.

A boat that carries someone's home
With freedom of canals to roam.
A bicycle clamped firm on top,
In case they need to find a shop.

Some boats sport bright gleaming paint;
Tubs of flowers and pictures quaint.
Others are more plain and lax
With piles of wood and coal in sacks.

Here and there a novice crew
Holiday for a week or two.
Carefully through locks they steer,
Scraping sides is what they fear.

Streetwise kids who are city bred
Shout out loud, "Mum, give us bread.
I want to feed the ducks and things
And see them flap their little wings."

As I pass the boats that stay,
The smell of cooking wafts my way.
Why is it when we are outdoors,
Others' food smells better than yours?

A boat with a neglected air,
Left as if no-one to care.
Grimy windows block the view;
A lucky horseshoe hangs askew.

Fancy names adorn the craft.
Some inspired and some plain daft.
"Firefly", "Witzend" to name but few
And made up ones like "Kenansu."

Seasoned travellers winch the gates
While chatting to their on board mates.
Others struggle with the chore;
It shows they've not done this before.

Dogs sit proudly in the bow;
They wish their friends could see them now.
New smells and noises, change of habit,
With luck the chance to chase a rabbit.

It's busy down beside the locks;
A place where everybody flocks.
Young and old, two legs or four,
Enjoy the peace, why ask for more?

Circus Magic

Colourful, vibrant, magical, twinkling
From the outside you don't have an inkling
Of the breath-taking sights that are inside the tent
Time spent at *Giffords* is money well spent

The minute you enter your world's upside down
Donkey and chicks roam with Tweedy the clown.
You soon are encompassed in their special world;
 Stories are told and tableaux unfurled.

Beautiful horses with riders to match;
Jugglers with fire can't afford not to catch.
Smart acrobats with limbs oh so supple;
Speciality act – a hand walking couple.

Regulars welcome old Brian the goose;
Many years now he has wandered round loose.
Not even upstaged by the big grizzly bear,
Suspiciously human, but we just don't care.

Musicians are splendid with such diverse skills;
An opera singer like a lark when she trills.
The piano is played with flair and panache;
The violin bow back and forth like a flash.

This magical troupe sweep you up with their verve;
Your senses are sharpened, you strain every nerve.
A frantic crescendo of music and dance;
Your hands smart from clapping at every last chance.

For just a short while you are lost in the glory,
Enjoying the sights and the smells and the story.
Faces all smiles, the occasional tear;
Starting to plan when to come back next year!

With thanks to Giffords circus for pulling out all the stops for me.

Photo credit to Mark Kent

Day Trip To Lacock

We'd promised ourselves an outing -
My husband, my daughter and me,
To visit a village of beauty
Owned by the National T.

The weather was pleasant and gentle,
The trees were of glorious hues;
We travelled through marvellous country
Affording spectacular views.

On arrival , we parked, then we pottered;
The village was charming and twee,
Cottages, cobbles and churchyards,
Hostelries, places for tea.

We enjoyed a tasty light luncheon
In a bar with a resident ghost
And looked at the local attractions,
Rural and home-made at most.

Then on to the abbey and cloisters,
In sizeable grounds, with a view,
Because I'm a bit short on breathing
They said, "It's a wheelchair for you."

I was helped to a chair that was handy
And of the collapsible kind,
Though that was a certain misnomer,
It was firmed by my ample behind!

We were off and into the garden,
And that's when they started to laugh;
Have you ever been bounced and gyrated
On gravel and uneven path?

My teeth they were rattling and shaking;
I hoped they were fixed in quite tight;
Perhaps with all the vibrations,
I'd rid me of some cellulite?

"Oh look at those marvellous gargoyles;
 Can you see, round the door there are two?"
But when you are all of a quiver,
There's certainly four in my view!

"An entrance with ramp, oh how thoughtful;
We can push you down there in a trice;
Oh sorry, I just hit the doorway.
Just settle back in now. That's nice!"

"Lets take you around in the garden;
You can see such a wonderful view;
Let's balance the chair on the ha ha"
('Spose you think that that's funny too!)

"We'll twirl you around on the pathway,
So you'll see through three sixty degrees."
Suddenly, you're part of a whirlwind,
Just a blur with the sky and the trees.

"We'd better turn back now, it's cooler.
Don't want you getting too chilled;
Sorry the ride is erratic,
These wheelchairs are sometimes self-willed."

Inside! The chair was prised from me,
The others were holding their backs,
"Hard work pushing these contraptions,
At least you could sit back and relax!"

We shuffled our way to the tearoom
And ordered a drink and a bun
And agreed that our little excursion
Had been a success and was fun.

If I Cannes You Can

I've been to Cannes (oh, not with a man!)
But just to see if the life is for me
I tried to pretend I had money to spend
So I stayed somewhere plush, with decor all lush
I walked up the drive, my bag by my side
And pretended my car had gone on afar
I held my head high when the porter was nigh
(My case he could see was not Louis V)
I was shown to my room and tried to assume
That I always lived well (d'you think they could tell?)
I partook of the wine, it went down just fine
A cocktail or two goes to soften the view
The waiters could charm, balance plates on their arm
And treat me with grace and a smile on their face
I went out to eat in a little side street
(Not 'cos it's cheap!) But on people to peep
There were men with flash cars looking handsome as stars
And girls in high heels with loud "arty" squeals
They had toy dogs for show and wouldn't let go
Of their gold plated leads – whatever their needs
I saw boats of such size they couldn't capsize
With bronzed men on deck washing down every speck
I gazed at the frocks, the prices were shocks
Said, "They're just not my style, in fact they're quite vile
And the jewellery my dear, far too common I fear,"
(You can't beat old Marks for some glitter and sparks)
At the end of my stay I just slipped away
No hoo-hah or fuss, nipped straight on the bus
But just for a while I'd lived in real style
And left as a fan of the high life in Cannes.

Opening Time

I think I'll have a biscuit with just a bite of cheese
I'll pop into the kitchen and help myself with ease.

Now will it be some cheddar or a piece of nice ripe brie?
With butter and some crackers and then a cup of tea.

I take a knife to slice it, the cheese is vacuum packed
But can I split the package? I try until I'm whacked.

I pick up a pair of scissors, a knife and razor blade
I hit the cheese in temper, now what a mess I've made.

I make a small incision, it feels like plasticine
And finally it oozes like something quite obscene.

Now it's time for biscuits, to open – tear the strip
But nowhere can I find it, it's getting on my pip.

I struggle with the wrapper, I'm tearing out my hair
Suddenly it opens – biscuits everywhere!

Let's calm the situation with a warm and soothing drink
Open the milk carton, contents – down the sink.

I settle for a fruit juice, a safer choice to make
The carton says, "On opening give a little shake."

I tip the carton quickly with an inadvertent squeeze
A shriek of indignation, orange covered knees.

Forget the bite of supper, now I need a shower
It shouldn't take too long now, back in half an hour.

I face a further challenge with the shampoo bottle cap
When at last I've finished I'm ready for a nap.

I take a glass of water, get ready for my bed
By now I need a tablet to cure my pounding head.

I settle on my pillows, pick up the tablet bottle
But I can't get it open; is there someone I can throttle?

Not Funny

I've lost my sense of humour
It's something I must find
If I can be this careless
I might just lose my mind.

I know I used to have one
'cos people told me so
I used to take it with me
Wherever I did go.

I've looked behind the telly
In case I left it there
I even watched some programmes
That only made me stare.

I had a sense of humour
For Manuel and John Cleese
I laughed at Del Boy Trotter
Falling down with ease.

I know I had it with me
When panel shows had wit
But alternative bad humour
Doesn't help one bit.

I often found it with me
When out with friends for dinner
These days if I just get there
I think myself a winner.

I know I used to use it
For witty repartee
But the audience has dwindled
Not what it used to be.

I had it in the summer
When the circus came to town
I gave it a good airing
At the antics of the clown.

I've laughed at the misfortunes
Of other people's pets
But now I tend to wonder
If they end up at the vets.

What happened to the custom
Of laughing till I cried?
When things were so amusing
A pain grew in my side.

I used to give out answers
With clever, sharp replies
Now I see the boredom
Show in people's eyes.

The things I now find funny
Are few and far between
For banana skin type humour
Miranda Hart is queen.

Maybe I've just lost it
Or it died from under use
Sense of humour failure
Subject of abuse.

If you know where I've left it
My sense of fun and witty
Just tell me and I'll claim it
And throw away this ditty.

written after a spell in hospital

Out On A Limb

My joints are refusing to bend
Oh I guess they'll give in in the end
But they're causing some moans
And plenty of groans
As into old age I descend.

I go to sit down in my chair
And hover a while in mid air
It seems a long drop
As I land with a plop
I'm really about to despair.

I bend to take things from a drawer
A task that is easy no more
I scrabble around
For things near the ground
With muscles exceedingly sore.

And what of the things on the shelf
I feebly reach to them with stealth
Jump up – make a grab
Like a sidewinder crab
It could seriously damage my health.

There are cobwebs hung over my stair
I certainly can't stand on a chair
I'll leave them a while
And then with a smile
I'll spray them at Christmas – with flair.

Kneeling is now out of bounds
Well not without tortuous sounds
Cos once on the floor
Well – you know the score
I could do with losing some pounds.

I try now to never be late
No rushing full tilt at the gate
Take a leisurely pace
Life isn't a race
No need to go tempting my fate.

So I'll try to stop sighing and groaning
And limit the volume of moaning
Like the Wimbledon stars
With their grunts, oohs and ahhs
I'll pretend it's my muscles I'm toning!

Produce Show

The day of the show dawned clear and bright
With only a wispy cloud in sight
Excitement ran through the Village Hall
The tension was mounting for one and all.

Weeks of preparing, digging, sewing
Would soon be judged and hope was growing
Who would gain the annual prize?
Winning by skill or taste or size.

Who produced the longest bean?
Whose apples had the rosiest sheen?
Whose bread was golden brown and crusty?
Who photographed old cycles – rusty?

Children from as young as two
Painted rainbows in each hue
Delightful gardens in a box
Complete with tiny veg and phlox.

Delicious looking chocolate cake
A section for the gents to bake
Rolls and flapjacks, tarts and scones
Which would be the winning ones?

Creative crafts were all displayed
Recycled items deftly made
Needlecraft and homemade wine
Guaranteed to taste sublime.

Dahlias in perfect bloom
A rose who's fragrance filled the room
Cups with flowers wound round their handles
A clever take on those four candles.

Tea was served with luscious cake
How much noise does chatter make?
Friends and neighbours all reflected
Could the winner be detected?

Awards were given on a card
Recognising who worked hard
Points awarded added up
To clarify who won the cup.

Congratulations – lots of cheers
A little rest before next year?
Eager entrants scanned the list
2015 would not be missed.

Lechlade's Annual Produce Show

Unscrooged

I was not a fan of Christmas I think it could be said
The fuss and the excitement made me shake my head
My Santa hat said, "Humbug" much to my friends delight
My Christmas decorations stayed hidden out of sight.

I didn't mind the shopping for presents for my friends
But I drew the line at joining in all the other trends
The festive Christmas music left me feeling cold
The thought of Christmas parties made me feel quite old.

But then one fated Christmas I really was quite ill
The doctors tried to cure me with every magic pill
Despite their ministrations they decided I should stay
A lengthy spell in hospital – right through Christmas Day.

I struggled through December each and every night
And didn't start improving till January was in sight
Santa didn't visit – I thought that was quite sad
A bit of ho ho ho-ing helps you feel less bad.

This year I started early and made a little list
I grabbed each opportunity, nothing would be missed
I made my cards and wrote them as early as I could
And smugly crossed the list off- I really felt quite good.

Next I bought my presents whenever I'd the chance
Friends all took me shopping to buy things in advance
I wrapped and sealed and labelled – humming all the while
The sound of Christmas music somehow made me smile.

I loved the decorations, the buzz and merry chatter
I even ate the mince pies though they make you fatter
I watched some Christmas telly though much we'd seen before
And watched for dear old Santa to pass by our front door.

This year on Christmas morning I took a different view
No more my grumps and humbug I knew what I must do
I laughed with all my family and toasted with good cheer
"A Merry Christmas everyone – at least this year I'm here!"

Pardon

I'm getting hard of hearing, have been for sometime
You need to speak quite clearly, might even add some mime
I used to laugh at Mother when asked her choice for tea
And roll my eyes to heaven when she answered, "Half past three."

I go with friends for dinner – in fact there's quite a crowd
All of them are speaking, it really is quite loud
But who knows what they are saying? I try to smile and nod
Expressions on their faces show they think I'm odd.

My Daughter comes to see me - quite softly spoken she
I'm sure she spoke much louder when she was only three
She sees my blank expression as we talk of this and that
And whispers to her Father, "Shame for the deaf old bat."

We have a lot of phone calls from youngsters in Mumbai
I'm justified in saying, "Can't hear you well – goodbye."
Close friends phone with some gossip, now this I just must tackle
But end the conversation with, "The line's bad with this crackle."

And as for TV programmes, my rantings know no bounds
I blame the background music, producer and the sound
There are films that I quite fancy but the words are such a jumble
Of course it's not my hearing, the actors all must mumble.

My husband asks a question, "Do you want a crumpet?"
I say, "Oh yes with jam on"- (he said a hearing trumpet!)
So if we meet by accident, not seen you for a while
Don't be exasperated by my enigmatic smile!

Shelf Life

Like a package on a shelf
Troubled no one, pleased myself
When all at once the words I hate,
"Better check her sell-by-date."

Surely not, they can't mean me?
'Cos I'm still fresh, why can't they see?
Ignore the wrinkles (laughter lines)
Memories of happier times.

There's still some tread left in my tyres
All of us can't be high fliers
Don't they know the oft heard rune?
Many old fiddles still play a good tune.

Packaging can oft tell lies
What's inside is the surprise
Although my wrappings old and tattered
Can it work is what once mattered.

But then of course that's what I see
In my mind I'm twenty three (?)
Let's face the facts, we know the score
I'm past the date I'm best before.

Nightmare

He came into the bedroom,
The stress showed on his face
He pursed his lips quite grimly
And then began to pace.

He mustn't let it rule him,
His intentions they were good
But the "thing" was there to haunt him,
He'd tame it if he could.

He'd approach this time quite gently
And coax it to behave
Not get into a temper
And like a loony rave.

In quiet contemplation
He hatched a cunning plan
The "thing" would soon be beaten
By one courageous man.

Should he make a sudden movement,
Attack by quick surprise?
Sometimes the sheer frustration
Brought moisture to his eyes.

At times his face was purple
And oaths and threats would spew
His wife just stood by helpless
There was nothing she could do.

He had to overcome this
To sleep at night in peace
A successful operation
Would be a great release.

He made a sudden movement
But was wrested to the floor
That wretched duvet cover
Had beaten him once more!

Johnny Depp Came To My Party

When Johnny Depp came to my party
It was a day I'll never forget
He was met with applause oh so hearty
The most stunning surprise I've had yet.

He came in the guise of Jack Sparrow
The pirate whose ship's The Black Pearl
My heart was as shot by an arrow
My senses were soon in a whirl.

He strolled straight to where I was sitting
And said, "There's no need for alarm,"
And presented some beautiful flowers
With a flourish and great deal of charm.

Excited and temporarily silenced
I'm sure that my mouth fell agape
As I looked at my friends stunned expressions
A great party feeling took shape.

I gazed at his handsome perfection
His eyes that were ringed round with kohl
Not once did he portray rejection
I felt sure he could see to your soul.

Like me, my friends all looked staggered
As he started to chat to them all
Off round the room he soon swaggered
And entertained all in his thrall.

We were treated to some belly dancing
And Jack Sparrow joined in with the troupe
He was gyrating, weaving and prancing
People all cheered with a whoop.

Another surprise entertainer
Was a cuddly pink Cheshire Cat
He joined in with Jack and the dancers
Nothing unusual in that!

Jack Sparrow was up to his antics
With a great deal of sway and panache
There were several potential crew members
Who'd be tied to the mast with a lash.

Eventually Jack had to leave us
We could only applaud and say thanks
But I'll bet with a snap of his fingers
We'd have willingly walked on the planks.

At the end of the day – reminiscing
We were all left under Jack's spell
We went home with pictures and stories
Eager to see friends and tell.

If I'm feeling a little downhearted
And my spirits are needing a pep
I just think of my marvellous party
And the day I met Jack/Johnny Depp!

With heartfelt thanks to Melo Sparrow the best Johnny Depp lookalike in the business

www.ingramcontent.com/pod-product-compliance
Lightning Source LLC
Chambersburg PA
CBHW072151200426
43209CB00052B/1125